MUSICA DEI DONUM

The series MUSICA DEI DONUM sets out to make accessible to performers a variety of interesting and generally less well-known vocal works. They are presented in practical format, with the aim of retaining a 'clean' text on the page; at the same time we have offered some performance suggestions for those who wish to consider them, placed in the vocal reduction. Whilst the reduction can be played on a keyboard, our priority has been to preserve the integrity of the vocal lines rather than to present an idiomatically pianistic score.

These editions have been prepared from original sources, brief details of which are provided, but this material is selective rather than comprehensive in scope. We prefer instead to offer something of real value to the performer: introductory comments which give an overview, surveying the piece from the vantage point of personal experience of the music in performance, and translations (commissioned especially for this series from Jeremy White) which aim to enable the performer to bring musical and verbal text into the same focal plane.

SALLY DUNKLEY & FRANCIS STEELE, 2007

EDITOR BIOGRAPHIES

T0056997

Sally Dunkley's interest in 16th-century vocal music was established during her years as a student at Oxford University, where she sang with the pioneering group the Clerkes of Oxenford and studied with its director, David Wulstan. Since then, her career as a professional consort singer has developed hand-in-hand with continuing in-depth study of the music as editor, writer, researcher, and teacher. The experience of working with several of the leading British groups in this area—she is a founder member of The Sixteen and sang over 1000 concerts with the Tallis Scholars—has afforded her unique insights into questions of performance practice. She has been involved in the preparation of practical scholarly editions over several decades and is increasingly engaged in sharing her experience through workshops and summer schools.

Francis Steele was born in Liverpool, the son of a docker. Christ's Hospital school nurtured his early musical interests, and while at Magdalen College, Oxford, he studied with David Wulstan and Dr. Bernard Rose, two remarkable mentors who combined scholarship with performance. This influence pervaded a singing career spanning nearly three decades, during which Francis sang with and furnished editions for the foremost British ensembles. Travelling and performing extensively, he has developed an intimate practical knowledge of Renaissance repertoire, and his main concern is an imaginative fidelity to musical and verbal text. Francis now lives at *La Maison Verte* in southern France, where he runs courses advocating this approach; he also coaches groups throughout Europe and in the USA.

Manuscript used for cover illustration © British Library Board. All Rights Reserved. (BL Shelfmark K.4.k.i)

FOREWORD

These settings of verses from Psalm 137 represent one of the most amazing musical exchanges in history. England was in a state of religious upheaval at this time and while Philippe de Monte was enjoying a lifetime of freedom to express his faith, William Byrd was living a life of suppression, unable to express his faith publicly. Byrd was only a young boy when de Monte came to England with Philip of Spain's chapel musicians, witnessing the brief reign of Mary and the resulting five-year return to Catholicism. However, thirty years later both were well aware of each other's faith and musical genius.

The setting by de Monte of the first few verses of *Super flumina Babylonis* is wonderfully eloquent, beautifully shaped and highly effective, but Byrd's response, *Quomodo cantabimus*, is all that and more. It is quite radically defiant with Byrd's plea to Catholics not to forget Rome so heartfelt that it is almost too much to bear. If these motets are performed together, without a break, that message cannot fail to be expressed.

HARRY CHRISTOPHERS, 2007

Harry Christophers conducts The Sixteen in performances of these motets on CORO 16001.

PREFACE

As a member of the choir of the private chapel of Philip II of Spain, Philippe de Monte (1521–1603) visited England in 1554 following the marriage of his employer to Queen Mary. It seems that he may have established some contact with the young William Byrd, for some 30 years later he sent to Byrd the eight-part motet *Super flumina Babylonis*, whose text may be interpreted as a barely veiled allusion to the dangerous situation that Byrd and his fellow Catholics faced under the Protestant regime in England.[1] De Monte set verses 1–4 (rearranging the order to 1,3,4,2) of that most famous psalm of captivity, and in the following year Byrd replied with *Quomodo cantabimus* (verses 4–7 of the same psalm). These details were recorded by the 18th-century antiquarian John Alcock, who wrote out both pieces in score in the manuscript London, British Library, Add.Ms.23624, presumably working from older partbooks.

That there is an intriguing historical and textual link between de Monte's and Byrd's settings of these verses is clear, but the question then follows of whether or not to perform them together. Issues of pitch,[2] and of the physical disposition of the singers—standing in double choir (de Monte) or in single (Byrd)—do arise, but are far from insoluble, as Harry Christophers' Foreword attests. Only a few editorial suggestions for dynamics seem necessary, as these essentially elegiac pieces flow naturally without imposed or extreme contrasts, following the ebb and flow of the phrases; more specific suggestions for phrasing are offered in the music examples of the Appendix. The most comfortable speed will of course depend on the size of performing ensemble and the acoustics of the building; for *Super flumina Babylonis*, ♩ = 75 is suggested as a starting point, and for *Quomodo cantabimus*, ♩ = 80.

SALLY DUNKLEY, 2007

[1] see Joseph Kerman, *The Masses and motets of William Byrd* (London, 1981), pp. 44–5.

[2] see David Wulstan, 'Byrd, Tallis and Ferrabosco', in *English Choral Practice 1400–1650*, ed. John Morehen (Cambridge, 1995), p. 127.

OXFORD

SSAATTBB choir, unaccompanied

Philippe de Monte

Super flumina Babylonis

William Byrd

Quomodo cantabimus

MUSICA DEI DONUM

Series Editors: Sally Dunkley & Francis Steele

TEXTS AND TRANSLATIONS

Super flumina Babylonis, illic sedimus et flevimus,
dum recordaremur tui Sion.
Illic interrogaverunt nos, qui captivos abduxerunt nos,
verba cantionum.
Quomodo cantabimus canticum Domini in terra aliena?
In salicibus in medio eius suspendimus organa nostra.

Quomodo cantabimus canticum Domini in terra aliena?
Si oblitus fuero tui, Jerusalem, oblivioni detur dextra mea.
Adhaereat lingua mea faucibus meis, si non meminero tui;
si non proposuero Jerusalem in principio laetitiae meae.
Memor esto, Domine, filiorum Edom in die Jerusalem.

By the streams of Babylon, there we sat and wept
when we remembered you, Sion.
There they questioned us, those who had led us into captivity,
about the words of our songs.
How shall we sing the Lord's song in a foreign land?
There on the willows we hung up our harps.

How shall we sing the Lord's song in a foreign land?
If I should forget you, Jerusalem, let my right hand fall idle.
Let my tongue stick in my throat if I do not remember you;
if I do not keep Jerusalem as the greatest of my joys.
Remember, Lord, what the sons of Edom did on that day in Jerusalem.

JEREMY WHITE, TRANS.

Super flumina Babylonis

PHILIPPE DE MONTE (1521–1603)
ed. Sally Dunkley

Súper flúmina Babylónis,
By the streams of Babylon,

illic sédimus et flévimus
there we sat and wept

Sally Dunkley has asserted her right under the United Kingdom Copyright, Designs and Patents Act, 1988, to be identified as the Editor of this work.

Copyright © 2007, Oxford University Press, Inc, assigned to Oxford University Press 2010.

Printed in Great Britain

dum recordarémur túi Síon.
when we remembered you, Sion.

-mus et fle - vi - mus, dum re -

-mus et fle - vi - mus, dum re - cor - da -

se - di-mus et fle - vi - mus, dum re -

et fle - vi - mus, et fle - vi - mus, dum re -

il - lic se - di-mus et fle - vi-mus, et fle - vi - mus,

et fle - vi - mus,

il - lic se - di-mus et fle - vi - mus,

fle - vi-mus, et fle - vi - mus,

Íllic interrogavérunt nos,
There they questioned us,

qui captívos abduxérunt nos,
those who had led us into captivity,

vérba cantiónum.
about the words of our songs.

Quómodo cantábimus
How shall we sing

55

cánticum Dómini in térra aliéna?

61 the Lord's song in a foreign land?

In salícibus in médio éius
On the willows there

suspéndimus órgana nóstra.
we hung up our harps.

Quomodo cantabimus

WILLIAM BYRD (1540-1623)
ed. Sally Dunkley

Quómodo cantábimus cánticum Dómini
How shall we sing the Lord's song

Sally Dunkley has asserted her right under the United Kingdom Copyright, Designs and Patents Act, 1988, to be identified as the Editor of this work.

Copyright © 2007, Oxford University Press, Inc, assigned to Oxford University Press 2010.

in térra aliéna?
in a foreign land?

oblirióni détur déxtra méa.
let my right hand fall idle.

Adháereat língua méa fáucibus méis,
Let my tongue stick in my throat,

si non meminero túi.
if I do not remember you;

Si non proposúero Jerúsalem
if I do not keep Jerusalem

in princípio laetítiae méae.
as the greatest of my joys.

Mémor ésto, Dómine,
Remember, Lord,

107

filiórum Édom
what the sons of Edom

113

in die Jerúsalem.
did on that day in Jerusalem.

44

EDITORIAL NOTES

Super flumina Babylonis

Sources

London, British Library, Add.Ms.23624, no.33, an 18th-century scorebook made by John Alcock.
London, British Library, Royal Music Library, Ms R.M.24.d.2, f.22v (John Baldwin's commonplace book);
 untexted except for incipit.
Two partbooks from the same set:
 The 'James' partbook (S2), f.112
 St Michael's College, Tenbury, Ms. 389 (A2), f.111
Prague, Národní Muzeum, MS XIV C 149, no.25 (A1); not consulted.

m.39ff :Though the sources give 'adduxerunt', we have followed the Vulgate's 'abduxerunt'. Either verb would make sense in the context: 'abduxerunt' as 'they led us away', and 'adduxerunt' as 'they led us to'.
m.21:S1 Baldwin specifies ♮, Add.23624 ♭
m.67 A1, B1; m.70 A2, B2; m.73 B1; m.74 A1 and T2; m.75 A2; m.76 A1, T1; m.82 A1, T2; m.83 A1, A2; m.84 A1, T1: Add.23624 gives ♭ to Es, resulting in a significantly different harmonic effect. This edition follows Baldwin, backed up by T389 (A2) which has no ♭ in m.70 or m.75 (unfortunately this manuscript omits mm.81–88 altogether, presumably in error).
m.91–92: The low A2 phrase may be sung by T2.

Quomodo cantabimus

Sources

London, British Library, Add.Ms.23624, f.123, an 18th-century scorebook made by John Alcock.
London, British Library, Royal Music Library, Ms.R.M.24.d.2, f.26 (John Baldwin's commonplace book);
 untexted except for incipit.
Two partbooks from the same set:
 The 'James' partbook (A1), f.114
 St Michael's College, Tenbury, Ms.389 (T1), f.114
Madrigal Society partbooks G.9-15, f.36v, and *Lbl* Add.Ms.34000, f.37v (S2 book of the same set)

In the first part of the motet, Bass 1 is followed in canon by Alto 1, and by Alto 2 in inversion.
Add.Ms.23624 reverses the two bass parts.
In the Madrigal Society partbooks, A1 becomes A2 and vice versa for the second part.
m95ff: Alcock consistently avoids the anacrusic underlay for 'laetitiae meae'.

I should like to thank the British Library for permission to publish these transcriptions from manuscripts in their collection.

SALLY DUNKLEY, 2007

APPENDIX

Super flumina Babylonis

Quomodo cantabimus

MUSICA DEI DONUM is a new early-music series that features a variety of lesser-known, interesting, and accessible works edited by early-music experts Sally Dunkley and Francis Steele. These editions have been prepared from original sources and are presented in a practical, uncluttered format. Performance suggestions appear in the vocal reduction, and running translations, commissioned especially for this series from Jeremy White, are positioned above each system for the edification and convenience of the performer.

Also from the MUSICA DEI DONUM series

Orlandus Lassus—Musica, Dei donum optimi

John Sheppard—Missa Cantate

William Mundy—Beatus et sanctus and Sive vigilem

MUSICA DEI DONUM

V- fica Dei donum optimi

OXFORD
UNIVERSITY PRESS

www.oup.com

ISBN 978-0-19-386817-5

9 780193 868175